MW01265580

Academy

SCIENTIFIC
AMERICAN

Volcanic Eruptions, Earthquakes, and Tsunamis

SCIENTIFIC
AMERICAN

Volcanic Eruptions, Earthquakes, and Tsunamis

By Sean McCollum

CHELSEA HOUSE
PUBLISHERS
An imprint of Infobase Publishing

Scientific American: Volcanic Eruptions, Earthquakes, and Tsunamis

Chelsea House
An imprint of Infobase Publishing
132 West 31st Street
New York, NY 10001

Library of Congress Cataloging-in-Publication Data
McCollum, Sean, 1963–
    Volcanic eruptions, earthquakes, and tsunamis / Sean McCollum.
        p. cm. — (Scientific american)
    Includes bibliographical references and index.
    ISBN-13: 978-0-7910-9047-3 (hardcover)
    ISBN-10: 0-7910-9047-7 (hardcover)
    1. Volcanic eruptions—Juvenile literature. 2. Earthquakes—Juvenile
        literature. 3. Tsunamis—Juvenile literature. I. Title. II. Series.
    QE522.M34 2007
    551.2–dc22   2007017740

Chelsea House books are available at special discounts when purchased
in bulk quantities for businesses, associations, institutions, or sales
promotions. Please call our Special Sales Department in New York at
(212) 967-8800 or (800) 322-8755.

You can find Chelsea House books on the World Wide Web at
http://www.chelseahouse.com

Series designed by Gilda Hannah
Cover designed by Takeshi Takahashi and Joo Young An

Printed in the United States of America

Bang GH 10 9 8 7 6 5 4 3 2 1

This book is printed on acid-free paper.

All links and Web addresses were checked and verified to be correct at
the time of publication. Because of the dynamic nature of the Web, some
addresses and links may have changed since publication and may no
longer be valid.

Contents

CHAPTER ONE

This Restless Planet

The ocean wind carried the stink of rotten eggs to the Iceland coast. Sensitive scientific instruments registered small earthquakes. The Icelanders recognized the signs: somewhere a **volcano** was spewing gases and preparing to erupt. The people there knew the destructive power of volcanoes. Several were active on their island country. But where was this one rumbling?

The crew of a fishing boat was the first to spot it on November 14, 1963: a plume of smoke and steam billowing out of the Atlantic Ocean. The volcano had been growing underwater 33 miles (53 kilometers) from Iceland's coast. Now the volcano's cone had reached the surface.

Scientists rushed to the spot to observe something they rarely had the chance to see: the fiery birth of a new island. For the next three years, this volcano erupted again and again. Sometimes it exploded and threw molten rock into the air. At other times, glowing orange **lava** oozed out and cooled into red-black rock. Each **eruption** created a new layer of land. In time, the volcano formed an island 1.7 square miles (2.7 km^2) in area and 300 feet (91 meters) high.

The new island was called Surtsey. Icelanders named it after Surtur, a fire giant of Icelandic myth.

Undersea volcanic eruptions near Iceland formed the island of Surtsey. These eruptions continued off and on from 1963 through 1967.

Earth's Supernatural Power

It's easy to understand why people link volcanoes and earthquakes to giants, gods, and other supernatural beings. The destruction caused by earth-shaking **seismic** activity can be beyond belief. (*Seismic* is the Greek term for "shaking.") For example, the force of the 1980 eruption of Mount St. Helens in Oregon was equal to a massive nuclear explosion. A powerful 1999 earthquake in Turkey killed more than 17,000 people. In 2004, a **tsunami**—a giant ocean wave launched by an undersea earthquake—destroyed towns and cities along the coasts of South Asia. More than 220,000 people died.

But volcanoes and earthquakes create as well as destroy. The island of Surtsey is one small example. Mountain ranges, pushed up when two landmasses collide, are much bigger ones. Earth's surface is slowly but constantly creating and remodeling itself. In the last 100 years, scientists have discovered more and more about how Earth does this. Their work is saving lives as it unlocks the secrets hidden far underground.

Unearthing Earth's Structure

The key to understanding volcanoes and earthquakes lies beneath the ground. For much of human history people assumed that Earth was solid rock through and through. But about 500 years ago, some wondered if the planet was mainly water with continents floating on top. Others observed lava bursting from underground and figured Earth's interior must consist of this fiery, melted rock.

It hasn't been easy to discover the truth. Earth is about 3,960 miles (6,378 km) from surface to center. Compare that to how deep humans have penetrated the Earth. The deepest cavers have ever crept and crawled is about 1.3 miles (2.08 km) underground. The deepest mine reaches down only about 2.5 miles (about 4 km). The deepest humans have ever drilled is about 9 miles

---

MYTHS FOR SHAKY GROUND

Today, people often look to science for answers about the world around them. But in the past, people often turned to myths—ancient stories that give supernatural reasons for natural events, including earthquakes and volcanoes.

In Japanese tradition, for example, earthquakes are caused by *namazu*—a giant catfish that lives in the mud beneath Japan. The Kashima god keeps the fish in check beneath a magic rock. But when the god lets down his guard the catfish thrashes around, shaking the earth. In the traditions of India, Australia, and the Americas, mythic animals are also the causes of seismic disasters.

Elsewhere, gods are held responsible. In Hawaii, the moody Pele is the goddess of volcanoes. When she stamps her feet in anger, says the legend, the ground moves and lava flows. The word volcano itself comes from Vulcan, the Roman god of fire, who is said to live in a volcano in Italy. There, in his fiery forge he hammers out weapons and armor for the other gods.

Lava from deep underground erupts in Iceland in 1973. The rock, minerals, and gases that reach the surface provide scientists with important information about Earth's interior.

(14.5 km) deep. When it comes to exploring our planet, humans have really only scratched the surface.

So how do scientists "explore" Earth's inner reaches where no one has ever set foot? They study rocks that have been pushed up from deep underground. They also drill into Earth's crust and bring up rock samples.

To investigate even deeper, researchers measure how vibrations, or **seismic waves**, move through the planet. They rely on sensitive instruments called **seismometers** to record and measure these vibrations. Seismic waves move at different speeds through different materials, giving clues about what's inside the Earth. In a way, this process uses sound waves to take an x-ray of the planet.

Based on their findings, **geologists** now think Earth consists of three main layers. On the surface is a hard and brittle **outer**

crust up to 50 miles (80 km) thick. This includes the continents and seafloor. Below that is the **mantle**, a thick, semi-fluid layer of solid and molten rock that reaches down 1,800 miles (2,900 km). And in Earth's center is the **core**, a ball of partly solid, partly molten iron and nickel measuring about 1,800 to 3,960 miles (2,900–6,378 km) in diameter. Temperatures there may exceed 9,000° F (5,000° C).

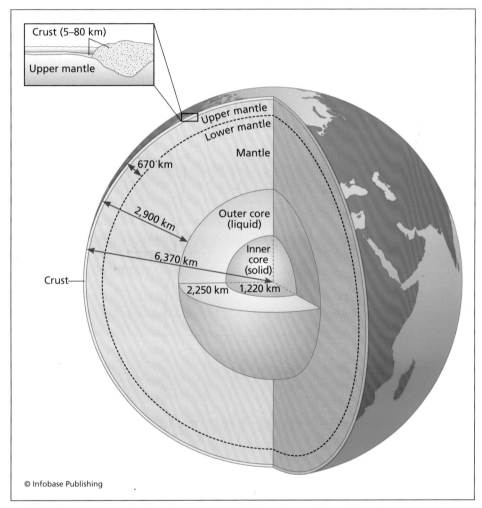

This diagram reveals Earth's structure. Scientists believe that the planet consists of a solid superheated core and a liquid outer core. The upper and lower mantles are thick, semi-fluid layers of rocks and minerals. Earth's crust is a thin, solid layer on the planet's surface.

The Global Puzzle

By the 1600s, explorers had mapped many of the globe's coastlines. Sharp eyes noted something: Africa's western hump seemed to fit nicely into the eastern gap between North and South America. And North America's East Coast seemed to match Europe's West Coast. Some geographers wondered if the continents had been pulled apart long, long ago. In 1620, English philosopher Francis Bacon wrote that the jigsaw-puzzle shapes of the continents were "no mere accidental occurrence." Bacon was not alone in wondering this.

During the 1800s and early 1900s, geologists and naturalists explored this theory. They collected more and more evidence that supported the idea that the continents had once been joined together. They recognized rocks in South America that were very similar to rocks in Africa. They identified identical animal species and fossils of ancient creatures on both continents as well.

Scientists offered various explanations. Some scientists speculated that catastrophic earthquakes or floods had wrenched

THE FATHER OF CONTINENTAL DRIFT

An experienced astronomer and meteorologist, Alfred Wegener (1880-1930) made many contributions to weather science. He was the first, for example, to use weather balloons to study air masses. But Wegener would make his biggest scientific contribution with his theory of continental drift.

Wegener first toyed with the idea around 1910. He proposed that the continents had been joined together tens of millions of years earlier, then drifted apart. He pointed to matching rock formations and fossils on distant continents as proof. "It is just as if we were to refit the torn pieces of a newspaper by matching their edges, and then check whether the lines of print run smoothly across," he argued. "If they do, there is nothing left but to conclude that the pieces were in fact joined in this way." Most Earth scientists of the time ridiculed the theory.

Wegener did not live long enough to enjoy credit for his ideas. He died at the age of 50 during an expedition across the Greenland ice cap.

entire continents and oceans to new locations. Others argued that at one time there must have been land bridges connecting the different continents. Plants and animals could have wandered across these links. They said that these land bridges must have later sunk into the ocean.

Other facts, though, were at odds with the land bridge idea. Scientists discovered fossils of warm-weather plants on the icy continent of Antarctica. They found evidence of glaciers in lands far too warm for them to exist today. This suggested that the continents themselves had moved from warm regions to cold regions, and vice versa.

In 1912, a German scientist named Alfred Wegener delivered a controversial theory: **continental drift**. He suggested that about 300 million years ago, all the continents were joined together. They formed a supercontinent, which he called **Pangaea**, a Greek term for "all earth." The continents then split apart and drifted away. Wegener suggested that the continents moved through the Earth's crust like ships plowing through ice.

Most geologists met Wegener's ideas with skepticism and even scorn. They argued that the continents were too soft to rip through the hard rocks of the ocean floor. And no one could imagine a force powerful enough to move the continents. Wegener could not come up with satisfactory responses to these doubts. He died without ever having won much support for his ideas.

New clues, though, were waiting on the ocean floor. Starting in the 1940s, new technologies such as sonar and submarines greatly advanced deep-sea exploration. One discovery was that the ocean floor wasn't smooth like the bottom of most lakes. The depths hid a lively landscape of undersea mountain ranges and deep trenches. This suggested that the ocean floor was not unchanging, but active and developing. Tests also showed that the ocean crust was much younger than scientists had thought.

In 1959, American geologist Harry Hess proposed an explanation for these discoveries: **seafloor spreading**. He speculated that magma was squeezing up through large ridges that had been

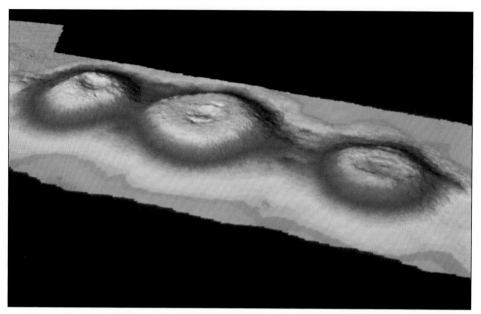

This image was made using sonar and echo-sounding technology, which bounces sound waves off the ocean floor. Located beneath the South Pacific Ocean, these underwater volcanoes are known as the Three Wise Men. Such volcanoes often develop near ridges where seafloor spreading occurs.

found in the ocean floor. The force pushed away the crust on either side of the ridge. Then the lava hardened into rock, creating a new section of crust. These undersea eruptions were repeated again and again over millions of years. Elsewhere, old crust was being forced back into deep undersea trenches.

Additional research supported the idea of seafloor spreading. In the 1960s and 1970s, a specially designed ship called the *Glomar Challenger* drilled into the ocean floor. It retrieved some 19,000 samples across miles of ocean. The farther the samples got from the volcanic ridges, the older the rocks were. In other words, the new crust was pushing older crust away from the ridge. Tests of the ocean floor's magnetic fields supported this idea.

All these findings confirmed the process of seafloor spreading. Earth is constantly churning out new crust through these ridges. Older crust is recycled back into the mantle in the deep-sea trenches.

Plate Tectonics

In the 1960s and 1970s, scientists brought together decades of geological research. They developed a description of how the surface of our planet works. It's called **plate tectonics**. (The term *tectonics* refers to Tekton, a gifted builder in Greek mythology.) Plate tectonics combined Wegener's ideas about continental drift with Hess's notion of seafloor spreading.

The theory of plate tectonics has established that the Earth's crust and uppermost mantle are broken up into about 15 pieces, or "plates." These plates move and jostle very slowly on a fluid layer called the **asthenosphere**. The continents, in turn, ride piggyback on the plates.

Tectonic plates move very, very slowly—at about the same rate as fingernails grow. But over millions and millions of years, those millimeters and inches add up to thousands of kilometers and miles.

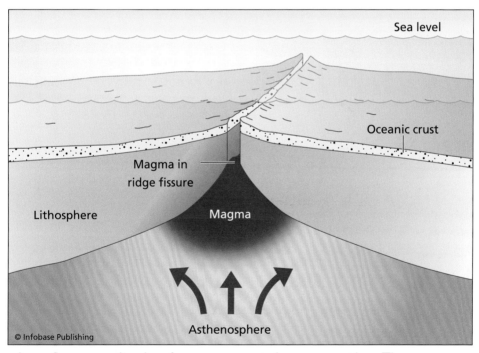

In seafloor spreading, lava forms new crust along ocean ridges. The crust then moves very slowly in opposite directions on both sides of the ridge. It is later recycled into Earth's interior in deep-sea trenches.

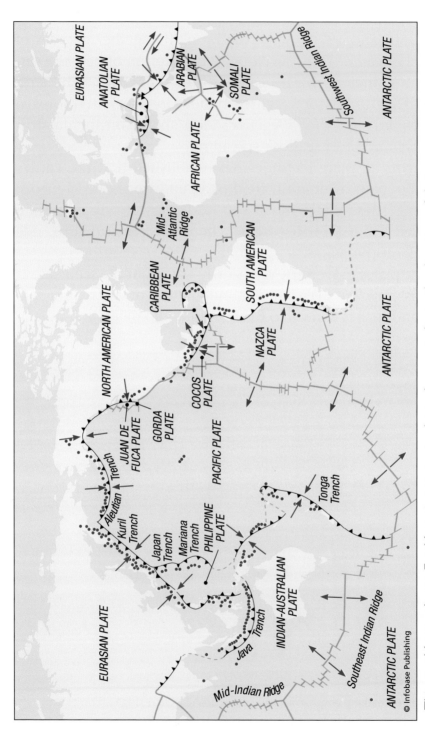

This world map shows Earth's major tectonic plates. Arrows indicate the direction of their movement. Most volcanoes and earthquakes occur where the plates grind against each other.

© Infobase Publishing

OUR FUTURE GLOBE

Plate tectonics are constantly remodeling our planet. But lucky for mapmakers, millions of years must pass before significant changes become noticeable.

The distant future will bring many changes to the globe's appearance. Among others, the Atlantic Ocean will become wider and the Pacific Ocean will narrow. Australia will move north and probably ram into Asia. A chunk of East Africa will begin to tear loose creating an inland sea. The coast of California will also pull away and drift north. Furthermore, the strip of land that connects North and South America will be pulled apart.

Hundreds of millions of years after that, the continents will all drift together to create a new supercontinent. Then they will move apart and wander away again.

Currently, scientists think there are two main forces driving plate movement. One is **convection**. The mantle beneath the plates circulates, fueled by heat from the planet's core. The mantle heats up near the core causing it to rise toward the Earth's crust. Near the surface and away from the heat source, it cools and flows downward again. The rising and falling goop in a lava lamp is a good example of convection at work. Inside the Earth, the convection of the mantle slowly drives plate movement.

Gravity also applies force on tectonic plates. In the deep-sea trenches, gravity pulls down on the leading edge of the plate that is sinking into the mantle. Ocean plates are heavier and denser than continental plates, so they always dive under continental plates. Like a tug on the edge of a tablecloth, the diving edge pulls the rest of the plate along with it.

We no longer think of Earth as a big, solid rock. Scientists now describe a dynamic planet that is constantly changing little by little. Where the planet's plates collide, grind together, and pull apart the world is its most restless. And that's where most volcanoes and earthquakes do their creating and destroying.

CHAPTER TWO

Volcanic Eruptions: When the Magma Rises

In May 1902, Mount Pelée started rumbling after centuries of sleep. The volcano overlooked St. Pierre, a city of about 28,000 people on the Caribbean island of Martinique.

Disaster loomed over this tropical paradise. On May 5, Pelée blasted a wall of hot water and debris down its side. Called a **lahar**, this fast-moving river of hot mud destroyed a factory and killed 23 workers.

Still, officials tried to reassure nervous residents that they had nothing to fear. To show their confidence, the island's governor and his wife traveled to St. Pierre on the morning of May 8.

They were never seen again.

Shortly after 8 A.M. that day, the mountain exploded. There was a bright flash and a deafening roar. The blast knocked people in St. Pierre off their feet. In an instant, a superheated wave of steam, ash, boulders, trees, and other debris hurtled toward the city. This wave, called a **pyroclastic flow**, reached speeds of up to 300 miles (500 km) per hour.

Within seconds, the pyroclastic flow tore into St. Pierre. The people there had no time to run and no place to hide. The surge

A volcano's pyroclastic flow can instantly bury entire communities. These people in Pompeii, Italy, were trapped by the eruption of Mount Vesuvius in 79 A.D. Archaeologists later uncovered their fossilized bodies.

snapped the lighthouse off its base. It shredded and flipped boats in the harbor. It ripped apart houses, office buildings, and stone churches like toys in a bully's sandbox.

Rescuers arrived by boat a short time later. They were greeted by an eerie quiet. They found two survivors. Everyone else—some 28,000 people—lay buried in the ruins of the city. It was the deadliest volcanic eruption of the twentieth century.

Volcanoes Defined

Volcanoes form any place where material from inside the planet reaches the surface. They draw life from miles beneath the Earth's surface. There, high temperatures create **magma**, a slow-moving fluid made of melted rock, gases, and minerals.

As magma nears the surface, there is less pressure pushing it down. This lets the magma rise faster. Less pressure also allows gases to escape from the super-hot mixture. If they find an opening to the surface, the magma and gases bubble or burst out to form a volcano. Once magma reaches the surface, it is called lava.

The power of the eruption depends on the kinds of gases released as well as the magma's thickness. The thicker the magma, the more difficult it is for gases to escape. This causes more and more pressure to build up. The higher the pressure is, the more violent the eruption.

Volcanologists sometimes compare volcanic eruptions to opening a can of carbonated soda. In their book *This Dynamic Earth: The Story of Plate Tectonics*, authors W. Jacqueline Kious and Robert I. Tilling wrote: "Such an explosive process can be compared to putting your thumb over an opened bottle of a carbonated drink, shaking it vigorously, and then quickly removing the thumb. The shaking action separates the gases from the liquid to form bubbles, increasing the internal pressure. Quick release of the thumb allows the gases and liquid to gush out with explosive speed and force."

Today, there are approximately 500 to 600 active volcanoes in the world. In addition, many undersea volcanoes still await discovery. An active volcano is one that has erupted sometime in

THE 10 DEADLIEST ERUPTIONS ON RECORD			
DATE	VOLCANO	LOCATION	DEATHS
A.D. 79	Vesuvius	Italy	16,000
1169	Etna	Italy	15,000
1661	Etna	Italy	20,000
1793	Unsen Island	Japan	50,000
1815	Tambora	Indonesia	12,000
1883	Krakatoa	Indonesia	36,000
1902	La Soufrière	Martinique	15,000
1902	Pelée	Martinique	28,000
1902	Santa Maria	Guatemala	6,000
1985	Nevado del Ruiz	Colombia	22,000

This "lava delta" was formed by pyroclastic flows on Montserrat Island. The volcano's 1995 eruption was its first in recorded history.

the last several thousand years. Many more volcanoes are considered dormant, or sleeping. They have not erupted in human memory, but someday they may reawaken. Lastly, there are extinct volcanoes—those considered unlikely to ever erupt again.

Types of Volcanoes and Powers of Destruction

Most land volcanoes are one of three basic types: composite volcanoes (often called stratovolcanoes), cinder cone volcanoes, or shield volcanoes.

Composite volcanoes, or stratovolcanoes, are the most recognizable, with their tall cone shape often topped with ice and snow. Japan's Mount Fuji and Mount Rainier near Seattle, Washington, are two famous examples. These volcanoes are built up by eruptions that spew out enormous amounts of rock and ash. They are considered the most dangerous type of volcano.

Cinder cone volcanoes are the most common type. They are smaller and less explosive than stratovolcanoes and usually erupt

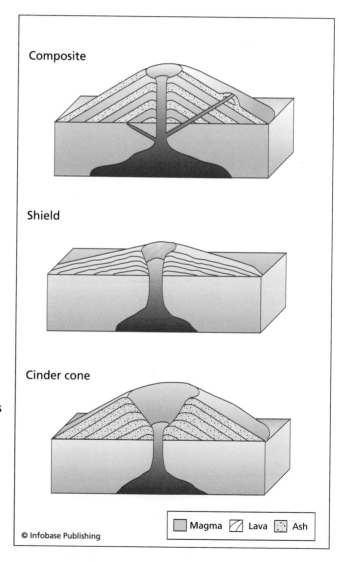

A volcano is any opening through which magma reaches the Earth's surface. A volcano's shape depends on the geology of the area, as well as the types of rock and gases the volcano ejects.

© Infobase Publishing

SUPERVOLCANOES

At first, people thought what they saw were simply large circular valleys, about 20 to 40 miles across (30-60 km). Then geologists went to work. They learned something startling. These land formations were actually **calderas** of gigantic supervolcanoes. The calderas were so big that people couldn't see them for what they actually were.

None of these supervolcanoes has erupted in human history. But if one ever does, scientists believe it would explode with the force of an asteroid smashing into the earth. It would blast and burn the landscape for many, many miles. The super-eruption would blanket huge areas with ash so heavy and thick that it could collapse roofs. For weeks, months, maybe years, ash and gases would block the sun and lower temperatures around the world. This could lead to starvation and the deaths of thousands or even millions of people.

Scientists have found four of these supervolcanoes so far. They include one beneath Yellowstone National Park in Wyoming and another in Long Valley, California. New Zealand and the island of Sumatra in Indonesia have the other two. None are threatening to erupt in the foreseeable future. But the potential power and destruction is so great that scientists are studying them with awe.

---

a single time. One or more may form around the base of a stratovolcano.

Shield volcanoes get their name from their shape. With their gradual slopes, they look like a warrior's shield set flat on the ground. Hawaii's Kilauea and Mauna Loa are both examples of shield volcanoes. Their explosions are rarely explosive, but they produce impressive shows of spraying and flowing lava.

Most volcanic destruction is not actually caused by lava. Red-hot lava will burn up and bulldoze anything it touches. But it usually moves so slowly that people and animals can easily escape. Buildings and other property, though, are not so lucky.

Volcanoes' most destructive punches almost always come from lahars and pyroclastic flows. Lahars, or volcanic mudslides, are caused when an eruption ejects water or instantly melts the

Kilauea volcano in Hawaii National Park begins to erupt in 1983. Lava flows in definite paths down its sides.

mountain's ice and snow. This can generate a massive flash flood and mudslide that wipes out anything in its path. Lahars can reach speeds of more than 60 miles (100 km) per hour.

A pyroclastic flow, like the one that destroyed St. Pierre, is also called *nuée ardente*, meaning "glowing cloud" in French. It is a giant, superheated blast of poisonous gas, rocks, ash, and other debris that nothing can withstand.

Where the Volcanoes Are Formed

Volcanologists have identified three areas in Earth's crust where volcanoes form: 1) along undersea ridges where the ocean floor is spreading; 2) along **subduction zones** where one tectonic plate is diving under another tectonic plate; and 3) in **hot spots** in the center of a tectonic plate.

Scientists are just beginning to understand volcanism as it relates to ocean-floor spreading. To study deep-sea volcanoes, scientists must descend miles under water in small submarines called submersibles.

There, undersea mountain ranges mark where two plates are separating. The Mid-Atlantic Ridge runs like a zipper through the Atlantic Ocean crust from north to south. Major ridges also exist in the Indian Ocean and the Pacific Ocean. As the plates move apart, mantle rock rises to fill the gap. This mantle rock melts and becomes lava when it oozes out to the ocean floor. Once the lava reaches water, it quickly cools and hardens, adding new rock to the Earth's crust.

Volcanoes caused by subduction zones are the most active and powerful. These zones, also called **convergent boundaries**, occur where the edge of an ocean plate is diving under a neighboring continental plate. Subduction zones are marked by deep undersea trenches.

Most scientists now think that the increased heat and pressure in subduction zones cause the sinking plate to release water. The water helps melt the rock in the mantle above the diving plate.

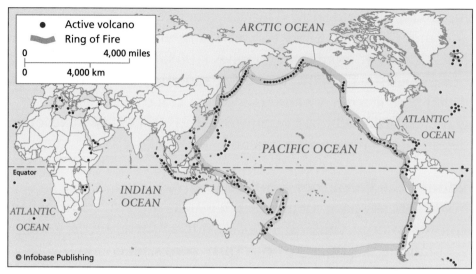

The "Ring of Fire" is where the Pacific Plate grinds against neighboring tectonic plates. The edges of this plate experience high levels of volcanic activity and earthquake risk.

This produces the magma that works its way through the continental crust to create volcanoes on land.

Subduction is responsible for much of the volcanic activity in the "Ring of Fire." This loop of volcanoes encircles much of the Pacific Ocean, dotting the coastlines of Asia, North America, and South America.

The third process that creates volcanoes is **hot spots**. In these places, magma rises easily to the surface. Plumes of super-hot magma burn through Earth's crust like a torch.

The Hawaiian Islands were created by such a hot spot in the Pacific Ocean. Geographers had noticed that these islands form an arc across 1,200 miles (1,900 km) of ocean. This island chain includes more than 50 volcanoes—some active, many extinct.

The research of Ian McDougall, an Australian scientist, added important knowledge to the understanding of hot spots. He found that the Hawaiian Islands to the northwest were older than those to the southeast. It was almost as if there was an undersea factory producing one island at a time. Then the islands seemed to be carried away as if on a conveyor belt.

In a sense, that is what is happening. Scientists have concluded that the Hawaiian hot spot is stationary. The Pacific Plate above it, however, is sliding across the hot spot very slowly. This process has produced one island after another during the course of millions of years. In fact, the hot spot is currently creating a new Hawaiian island—called Loihi. Experts think it will reach the ocean surface sometime in the next 20,000 years.

Mount St. Helens: Timeline of an Eruption

In 1980, Mount St. Helens erupted with even more power than Mount Pelée. But because of its location, new scientific knowledge, and early warnings, the results were much different.

Along the northwest coast of the United States, the Juan de Fuca Plate is subducting beneath the much larger North American Plate. There the mantle melts into magma and forms volcanoes in the crust above. Over millions of years, this process has produced Mount Shasta, Mount Rainier, Mount Hood, Mount St. Helens, and other majestic peaks.

These snow-capped mountains appear grand yet peaceful. Sometimes it is easy to forget that they are active volcanoes. But

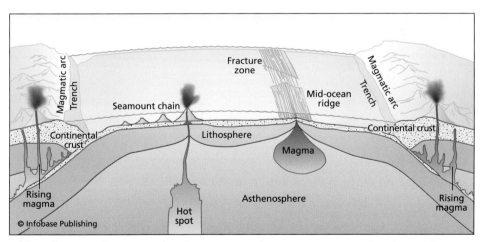

This diagram illustrates the three types of areas prone to volcanic activity: subduction zones, where two plates collide; a mid-ocean ridge, where two plates pull apart; and a hot spot, where magma melts through the crust.

Mount St. Helens reminded the world of its true nature in 1980. It had not erupted in 123 years. In March 1980, though, the mountain woke up.

The first signs were frequent small earthquakes in the area. These tremors signaled that magma and gases were rising. Teams of scientists flocked urgently to Mount St. Helens. They set up sensors to monitor the quakes and watched for clues that an eruption was about to happen.

The first eruption took place on March 27, 1980. It blasted steam and ash nearly 6,500 feet (2,000 m) into the sky. For the next two weeks the volcano occasionally released gases and ash. Then all volcanic activity stopped.

Between May 7 and May 16, Mount St. Helens released more steam. Observers noted a growing bulge on the peak's northern

The 1980 eruption of Mount St. Helens released more energy than any bomb human beings have ever exploded. The explosion, pyroclastic flow, and lahars devastated thousands of square miles of forest and blanketed the region in gray ash.

THE YEAR WITHOUT A SUMMER

In 1815, Tambora erupted in the Asian country of Indonesia. Scientists think it may have been the most powerful eruption in recorded history—much greater than that of Mount St. Helens. Tambora's blast killed some 12,000 people.

The terrible effects, though, were not just felt in Indonesia. The eruption sent tons of ash and gases high into the atmosphere. Air currents carried them around the world. Volcanic particles blocked out the sun. Sulfur dioxide, a volcanic gas, reflected the sun's heat back into space.

Without the sun's full energy, the year 1816 was much cooler in North America. Cold, frost, and snow killed crops and left people starving. A June blizzard dropped six inches of snow in New England.

That year went down in history as "The Year Without a Summer." It demonstrated the global reach of volcanoes' awesome power.

side. The bulge suggested that a surge of magma was building up there.

On May 18, volcanologist David Johnston woke up to a sunny day. He aimed his binoculars at Mount St. Helens from about six miles (10 km) north of the mountain. At 8:30 A.M., an earthquake rocked the area. The disturbance caused the bulge to collapse. Gases and magma under high pressure suddenly had an opening. They erupted from the side of the mountain with incredible force. "This is it!" Johnston radioed to his research base.

Within 10 minutes, the eruption's billowing cloud had reached nearly 12 miles (19 km) into the sky. A pyroclastic flow tore across neighboring hills and valleys. The sudden heat instantly melted the ice and snow. The water gushed down the mountainside, producing massive lahars that buried the forest landscape in gray mud.

When the smoke cleared, almost 1,000 feet (300 m) had been ripped off the top of Mount St. Helens. Volcanic ash fell like snow for hundreds of miles. Millions of trees lay flattened and burned on the scorched landscape. Property damage totaled $1.1 billion.

Dr. David Johnston uses a correlation spectrometer to measure ultra-violet radiation as an indicator of the sulfur dioxide content of gases released from Mount St. Helens in 1980.

As destructive as the eruption was, though, only 57 people died. Most collapsed after getting trapped in the volcano's poisonous gas. But close monitoring by scientists and officials kept the number of deaths from being much higher. Their early warnings had given people enough time to **evacuate** the area safely.

One of the dead was volcanologist David Johnston. Today, a research station in Mount St. Helens Volcanic Monument is named for him.

CHAPTER THREE

Earthquakes: Shocks from Underground

In the early morning of April 18, 1906, the people of San Francisco got the rudest of wake up calls. The strange whining and yapping of dogs had already awakened some of them. At the fire department, the horses went berserk and broke down their stalls. Then came a low rumbling sound.

About 5:12 A.M., the earthquake struck. The ground heaved and shook like a live animal. People were thrown from their beds. One woman reported that "the . . . trees [were] rising and falling on each wave, like ships at sea. . . ." Buildings twisted, toppled, and sank into the ground.

The shaking only lasted about 45 seconds. The destruction, though, was far from over. The quake had toppled stoves and ruptured underground gas pipes. Fire quickly spread. At the same time, the water mains had burst, so there was nothing to fight the flames with. For three days, San Franciscans watched helplessly as most of their city burned. Historians believe that more than 3,000 people died.

For seismologist Harry Fielding Reid, though, inspiration rose from the ruins. Before the quake, the land around San Francisco had twice been carefully surveyed. Reid checked these reports and

The 1906 San Francisco earthquake and fire destroyed much of the city. Yet, the disaster led to new discoveries in quake and science safety.

found that streams, fences, and roads that crossed a certain strip of land—the San Andreas Fault—had been gradually bending before the quake. After the quake, a new survey was done. This time, measurements showed that the same streams, fences, and roads had split apart or shifted dramatically. In some places, the land had slipped as much as 21 feet (7 m). These findings gave Reid a breakthrough idea about the causes of earthquakes.

In some parts of the globe, earthquakes are common events. The United States Geological Survey estimates that more than 3 million quakes take place worldwide each year. That equals 8,000 earthquakes a day. Most are so small that people do not feel them, and only sensitive measuring devices even register them. Some larger quakes do little damage because they rock the ground far from where people live.

Major earthquakes, though, are easily the most destructive of all natural disasters. In the last 100 years, they have resulted in the deaths of some 1.5 million people and billions of dollars worth of property damage. Those who survive a powerful quake often describe it as the most terrifying experience of their lives. But until the last century, the whys, wheres, and hows of earthquakes escaped scientific understanding.

THE 1906 SAN FRANCISCO EARTHQUAKE, A FIRST PERSON ACCOUNT

Earthquakes can be hard to imagine for people who have never experienced one. Here is an excerpt from Emma M. Burke's account of San Francisco's 1906 earthquake.

> We braced ourselves in the doorway, clinging to the casing. Our son appeared across the reception room, and my husband motioned to him to stand in his door also, for fear of the chimney [falling through the ceiling].
>
> It grew constantly worse, the noise deafening; the crash of dishes, falling pictures, the rattle of the flat tin roof, bookcases being overturned, the piano hurled across the parlor, the groaning and straining of the building itself, broken glass and falling plaster, made such a roar that no one noise could be distinguished.
>
> We never knew when the chimney came tearing through; we never knew when a great . . . picture weighing one hundred and twenty-five pounds crashed down, not eight feet away from us; we were frequently shaken loose from our hold on the door, and only kept our feet by mutual help and our utmost efforts, the floor moved like short, choppy waves of the sea, crisscrossed by a tide as mighty as themselves. . . . I never expected to come out alive. I looked across the [room] at the white face of our son, and thought to see the floors give way with him momentarily. How a building could stand such motion and keep its frame intact is still a mystery to me.

The Power of Plates and Slipping Faults

Earthquakes are caused by sections of the Earth's crust getting stuck and then unstuck. That was Harry Fielding Reid's ground-breaking idea. The Earth's tectonic plates move at a slow but steady rate. But along the edges, the plates do not always slide smoothly. Their edges get caught on each other. The rest of the gigantic plate, though, continues moving. Stress builds up and the ground stretches as much as it can. This explained the bending of the ground Reid noted when he compared the two surveys done before 1906.

Earthquakes are triggered when the force of the moving tectonic plates overcomes the **friction** that locks the edges together. Then the sections lurch abruptly to catch up with the rest of the plate. In a way, earthquakes are like when a person pushes against a stuck door. The harder the person has to push, the more energy gets stored up. When the door pops loose, the energy is released, and the person lurches forward. Likewise during an earthquake, if a lot of energy has been stored up, the crust lurches violently. It sends waves of energy flowing through the ground in the form of earthquakes.

Earthquakes often happen in a series. The series might begin with smaller tremors known as **foreshocks**. The biggest quake in a sequence is called the **mainshock**. This is usually followed by **aftershocks**—multiple but less powerful tremors that may hit hours and days after the mainshock.

Reid's research did more than present a basic model of what causes quakes. It also helped make the case for plate tectonics. By analyzing where quakes occur most often, scientists have been able to trace the outlines of the Earth's tectonic plates.

Faults and Waves

Almost all earthquakes occur in fault zones. **Faults** mark boundaries where tectonic plates grind against each other. Scientists categorize three main types of faults: normal faults, thrust faults,

California's San Andreas Fault stretches from north of San Francisco to near the border with Mexico. In some parts of the fault, the rift is dramatically visible on the surface.

and transform, or strike-slip, faults. The type of fault depends on how the plates interact.

In a **normal fault**, the break is almost straight up and down. The moving tectonic plates pull apart, and one side slides down the other.

In a **thrust fault**, the two sections of crust are colliding. When the locked crust breaks free, one side is forced up the side of the other.

In a **transform**, or **strike-slip**, fault, one section of crust drags along the side of another section, like a sideswiping car. This

These are block models of the three most common faults. A strike-slip fault acts like two side-swiping cars. In a normal fault, one side slides down the other. In a reverse fault, one side gets pushed up the side of the other.

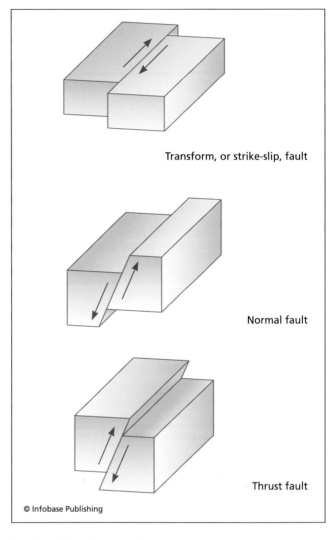

Transform, or strike-slip, fault

Normal fault

Thrust fault

© Infobase Publishing

is the least common kind of fault. California's San Andreas Fault, though, is a famous example of a strike-slip fault.

The San Andreas Fault runs for 650 miles from north of San Francisco to near the border of Mexico. Here, the Pacific Plate is moving to the northwest. The North American Plate is moving to the southeast. When sections get stuck together, stress builds. The contest between the two plates has also caused smaller faults in the crust that have spread out like cracks in a windshield.

Earthquakes occur when these stuck edges suddenly break free. This sends vibrations called **seismic waves** racing through the ground. The waves move away from the quake like ripples from a rock splashing in a pool.

These quake waves take different forms. The first two are known as **body waves** since they move through the body of the Earth. The first and fastest body wave is called the **primary wave,** or **P wave**. P waves stretch and compress the ground like an accordion. People usually feel these as a kind of thud.

Close behind P waves come **secondary waves,** or **S waves**. These usually move sharply up and down or from side to side, like a jump rope being whipped.

The waves that follow are known as **surface waves** because they travel along the Earth's surface. They are slower than body waves and cause the most vibration and damage.

Finding and Measuring Quakes

For seismologists, seismic waves help pinpoint where an earthquake started. The underground point where a fault first breaks loose is called the **focus**. The point on the Earth's surface directly above that is known as the **epicenter**.

When a wave arrives at a seismic station, a seismograph records the time and wave strength. Because researchers know the speed of P waves, S waves, and surface waves, they can calculate the distance between the seismograph and the earthquake's focus. By comparing when the waves reach a seismic station, seismologists can calculate what part of the fault triggered the quake.

Seismographs also record an earthquake's power. A quake's **magnitude** is a measurement of the amount of ener-

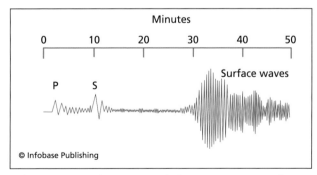

A seismograph registered this seismogram of an earthquake. By recording each wave's arrival time on a seismograph, scientists can calculate the earthquake's focus, or starting point.

A 1960 earthquake in Chile registered a magnitude 9.5 and caused extensive damage. This quake remains the most powerful on record.

gy a quake releases. It depends on how many miles of the fault ruptured, or broke loose, and how much energy the fault had built up. The **Richter scale** is the most familiar system for computing the magnitude of an earthquake.

Earthquake magnitude scales can be a challenge to understand. They use a mathematical formula called a logarithm to measure earthquake power. In practice, a magnitude 5.0 earthquake is not simply one step more powerful than a 4.0 quake. When measuring earthquakes, an increase of 1 magnitude equals 10 *times* more ground motion. It also means a jump of about 32 in a quake's power. Therefore a magnitude 5.0 earthquake is 32 *times* more powerful than a 4.0 earthquake. And a 6.0 earthquake is 32 *times* more powerful than a 5.0. So a 6.0 magnitude earthquake is more than 1,000 times (32 × 32 = 1,024) more powerful than a 4.0 earthquake.

People usually do not feel an earthquake that is less than magnitude 2.5 to 3.0. But anything over magnitude 6.0 has the potential to do great damage. Seismologists estimate that the 1906 San Francisco earthquake was about magnitude 7.8. The most powerful quake ever recorded took place in Chile in 1960 and registered a magnitude of 9.5. The level of destruction, though, depends on whether or not the quake hits near a city.

Danger Zones

As mentioned earlier, most earthquakes occur where Earth's massive tectonic plates collide. The Ring of Fire that marks the rim of the Pacific Ocean is one of the most active zones. The powerful quakes that rock Alaska, the California coast, South America's west coast, Indonesia, the islands of Japan, and the Philippines,

EARTHQUAKE MAGNITUDE AND CHARACTERISTICS

Richter Magnitude	Surface Wave Height (in feet)	Length of Fault Affected (in miles)	Diameter Area Quake Felt (in miles)	No. of Quakes per Year
9.0	Largest earthquakes ever recorded			
8.0	300	500	750	1.5
7.0	30	25	500	15
6.0	3	5	280	150
5.0	0.3	1.9	190	1,500
4.0	0.03	0.8	100	15,000
3.0	0.003	0.3	20	150,000

10 DEADLIEST EARTHQUAKES IN HISTORY

Date	Location	Magnitude (if available)	Death Toll
1556	Shenshu, China		830,000
1976	Tangshan, China	7.6	650,000
1737	Calcutta, India		300,000
1803	Tokyo, Japan		200,000
1927	China		200,000
1920	Kansu, China	8.6	180,000
1923	Tokyo and Yokohama, Japan	8.3	143,000
1857	Tokyo, Japan		107,000
2005	Pakistan	7.6	73,000
1908	Messina, Sicily	7.5	73,000

are all products of the movements of the Pacific Plate and its neighboring plates.

Another band of high seismic activity runs for 2,500 miles from eastern Asia to southern Europe. Here, multiple tectonic plates contribute to the restless crust. They are the source of earthquakes in Italy, Greece, and other countries around the Mediterranean Sea. The band also runs through Turkey and other parts of Central Asia.

Farther east, the tectonic plate carrying India and Australia is plowing into southern Asia. This collision of plates forces Earth's crust skyward. One result is the majestic Himalayan Mountains—the tallest peaks in the world. Another consequence is frequent earthquakes. With the dense population of people in countries such as India and China, quakes there are often deadly. Asia suffers from the destructive power of earthquakes more than any other continent.

CHAPTER FOUR

Tsunamis: Killer Waves

Tilly Smith noticed something weird. The 11-year-old British girl watched as the ocean seemed to drain quickly from the beach. "I noticed that . . . the sea was all frothy like on the top of a beer," she told the British Broadcasting Corporation. "It was bubbling." Sunbathers wandered out to look at the flopping fish and other undersea creatures exposed by the retreating water.

Then Tilly remembered a school geography lesson from two weeks earlier. She had seen a video about a tsunami, a killer ocean wave. She instantly realized that her family and everyone near the beach were in danger.

It was the morning of December 26, 2004. Tilly and her parents and sister had been soaking up the sun during their vacation in Thailand. This Asian country juts out into the Indian Ocean. At that moment, waves of incredible power were already speeding toward them.

Tilly had recognized the signs and knew what would follow. "I said, 'Seriously, there is definitely going to be a tsunami'," Tilly recalled. At first her parents were slow to believe her. Then her

The tsunami that hit southern Asia on December 26, 2004, wiped away coastal villages and killed more than 200,000 people. These islets used to be part of Banda Aceh, the capital city of Indonesia's Aceh province.

dad told a security guard. The alert quickly spread up and down the beach. People ran inland. Tilly's family climbed to the third floor of their hotel.

Minutes later, a wall of unstoppable ocean swept over that beach and other Indian Ocean coastlines. More than 220,000 people were killed. Millions more were left homeless. It was one of the most destructive natural disasters in human history. Thanks to Tilly and her geography lesson, though, her family and others at the beach escaped with their lives.

Tsunamis are powerful waves that can travel at high speeds across thousands of miles of ocean. *Tsu nami* is Japanese for "harbor wave," and Japan has experienced more than its share.

Fortunately, tsunamis are rare. Every year about two of these waves do some local damage. About every 15 years, a major tsunami strikes coastlines across a wide region. Eighty-five percent of tsunamis occur in the Pacific Ocean. They are difficult to detect before they reach land, which can make them deadly. The

2004 tsunami took a terrible toll, but it also gave scientists their best chance yet to study this force of nature.

Tsunami Triggers

Tsunamis are triggered by any event that displaces, or moves, enormous amounts of seawater. Earthquakes on the ocean floor are the most common cause of tsunamis.

Most of these underwater quakes happen at subduction zones—the boundaries where the heavier ocean tectonic plate plunges beneath a continental plate. As the lower plate slides under the upper plate, the edges get stuck. Eventually, the edges snap free and release energy in the form of earthquakes, as described in Chapter Three.

Quakes from underwater normal and thrust faults are the main seismic sources of tsunamis. In both of these, a section of crust lurches up or down. When a submarine earthquake strikes, a large section of seafloor may buckle this way. This displaces massive amounts of water, which may give birth to a tsunami.

MAJOR TSUNAMIS SINCE 1990

Date	Location	Max. Wave Height	Fatalities
Dec. 26, 2004	Indian Ocean	100 feet (30 m)	about 230,000
June 23, 2001	Peru, south coast	15 feet (4.6 m)	26
July 17, 1998	Papua New Guinea	50 feet (15 m)	more than 2,200
Feb. 21, 1996	Peru, north coast	16 feet (5 m)	12
Feb. 17, 1996	Irian Jaya, Indonesia	25 feet (7.7 m)	161
Jan. 1, 1996	Sulawesi, Indonesia	11 feet (3.4 m)	9
Oct. 9, 1995	Jalisco, Mexico	36 feet (11 m)	1
Nov. 14, 1994	Mindoro Island, Philippines	23 feet (7 m)	49
June 2, 1994	East Java, Indonesia	46 feet (14 m)	238
July 12, 1994	Okushiri, Japan	101 feet (31 m)	239
Dec. 12, 1992	Flores Island, Indonesia	85 feet (26 m)	more than 1,000
Sept. 2, 1992	Nicaragua	33 feet (10 m)	170

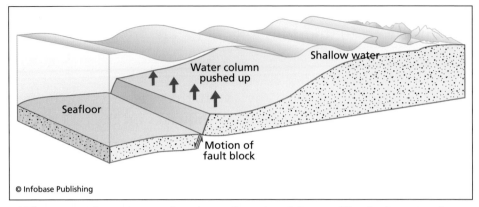

When an underwater earthquake strikes, the violent uplift of a huge section of seafloor may set a tsunami in motion. These giant waves travel at high speeds and hit coastal areas with tremendous force.

Earthquakes, though, are not the only source of tsunamis. Violent volcanic eruptions can also set the powerful waves in motion. Some scientists believe that an underwater pyroclastic flow from Krakatau's 1883 eruption launched a wave as tall as a 12-story building. That tsunami killed more than 30,000 people in Indonesia.

Researchers are also investigating how underwater landslides can trigger tsunamis. A small earthquake or other disturbance may send tons of rocks and mud skidding down a deep-sea slope. If the landslide is big enough, it can shove enough water to create the fast, deadly waves. An underwater landslide, disturbed by a magnitude 7.1 earthquake, is the suspected cause of a 1998 tsunami in Papua, New Guinea. That killer wave killed more than 2,200 people.

December 26, 2004

Tsunamis include three stages: **generation**—the earthquake or other event that causes it; **propagation**—how the waves move or spread; and **inundation**—the flooding when the tsunami hits land.

The generation of the 2004 Indian Ocean tsunami began on December 26 at 7:59 A.M. local time. That's when an earthquake

After the 2004 tsunami struck land, this car was lifted into a river, which drained after the tsunami hit, in Khao Lak, Thailand.

struck in a fault off the coast of Sumatra. A 750-mile (1,200-km) section of seafloor violently lurched upward by as much as 26 feet (8 m). This sudden shift catapulted billions of cubic feet of water into motion.

A global network of seismic stations soon sensed the powerful quake. Researchers, though, could not confirm that a tsunami was on the move. And even if they had known for sure, there was no system in place to warn people in the tsunami's path.

The tsunami's propagation, or spread, was astonishingly fast. The first waves raced through the Indian Ocean at speeds worthy of a commercial jet—about 300 to 600 miles (500 to 1,000 km) per hour.

In the deep ocean, a tsunami may be barely noticeable. At such depths of water, a tsunami's energy and shape are spread throughout a vast volume of water. Sailors might not even feel its waves pass beneath their boat.

But a powerful tsunami has global reach. Within 20 minutes of the quake, the December 2004 tsunami blasted the northern

TSUNAMIS FROM OUTER SPACE

The movie *Deep Impact* shows another cause of tsunamis: large asteroids or comets from space splashing into the ocean. In the movie, a giant comet of ice and rock hurtles toward Earth. A huge piece of it smashes into the Atlantic Ocean. The collision blitzes the eastern United States and other coastlines with mountains of water.

Such collisions have occurred in Earth's ancient past. Geologists have found proof of the resulting tsunamis by digging down and studying **sediment**—sand, rocks, and other deposits—on land.

Researchers in Texas found such marine deposits far inland where the ocean had never reached. They concluded that a tsunami had carried the sediments there. Their work helped locate a giant crater in the Gulf of Mexico where an asteroid crash-landed about 65 million years ago. That impact may have caused environmental changes that led to the extinction of the dinosaurs.

But no giant space rocks have struck Earth in human history—except on the movie screen.

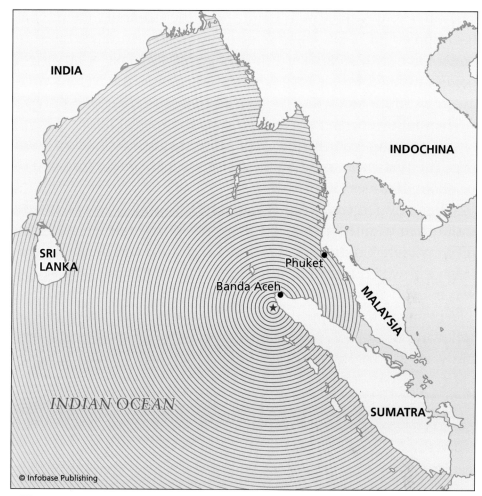

This computer-generated model shows the waves of the December 2004 tsunami just as they reach Sri Lanka. The giant waves raced out from a magnitude 9.0 quake, which struck near the city of Banda Aceh.

coast of Sumatra. Within three hours it reached the coasts of Thailand, Myanmar, and Malaysia to the east, and Sri Lanka and India to the west. Within 11 hours, the wave traveled 8,000 miles west to South Africa where it was blamed for at least one death. Eventually, the fading tsunami reached all the way to the eastern shores of South and North America.

Inundation or flooding is a tsunami's last stage. That is when it wreaks destruction on land. As the waves approach a coastline, the water grows shallower. Until then, the tsunami's energy has been spread out. Now the shallower water concentrates the tsunami's force into a smaller and smaller space. Like a lazy river being funneled into a narrow stretch of rapids, the water's energy grows more focused.

The shallower water also slows down the wave. But faster water is still pushing from behind. The water begins to "pile up" and rise. The first wave to hit Sumatra, for example, was estimated to be about 100 feet (30 m) tall.

When the December 2004 tsunami hit land, it swept inland more than a mile. It snapped trees, bulldozed homes, and toppled concrete buildings. It lifted cars and ships and dragged them inland. It wiped away entire villages. The death and destruction was beyond belief.

When a rock is dropped in a pool, it causes rings of ripples, one following the others. A tsunami's series of waves spreads in a similar way. But the waves of a tsunami may arrive many minutes

This illustration hints at a tsunami's power. In deep water, a tsunami may be barely noticeable. But once it reaches shallower water near land, the waves slow down and rise, creating an irresistible wall of water.

A DISASTER'S SILVER LINING

Aceh (AH-chay), on the Indonesian island of Sumatra, was one of the areas hardest hit by the December 2004 tsunami. More than 30,000 people died in that region. The disaster, though, may have had a silver lining for the people there. It helped bring an end to a 30-year-old war.

The Free Aceh Movement had been seeking independence from Indonesia. But after the tsunami, the group declared a ceasefire. They accepted help from the Indonesian government and international aid groups. The cooperation led to a peace agreement in August 2005.

apart. Often unsuspecting people return to the water's edge after the first wave hits, only to be caught off-guard and washed away by the next.

Tsunami-Ready

Just three months after the December 2004 disaster, another strong earthquake struck. It tore at the same underwater fault near Sumatra. This time, the results were much different. The quake occurred under shallower water. That meant less water was displaced when the seafloor shifted. And the island of Sumatra blocked much of the tsunami from hitting Thailand and other coastal countries.

Also, people near the quake's epicenter immediately ran inland as soon as they felt the ground shake. They had learned that a tremor might signal an oncoming tsunami. All these factors added up to a lower death toll.

Both Tilly Smith's warning and the March 2005 tsunami demonstrated an important point. When it comes to natural disasters, education is the best bet to save lives. If people in tsunami-prone areas can recognize danger signs—such as an earthquake or retreating water—they improve their chances of escape. If they plan and mark escape routes for their community, they will increase their odds of survival.

CHAPTER FIVE

Building for
"The Big One"

With a thud, the two-story white house shudders, then begins to sway. The hanging light swings wildly. Lamps and a computer screen pitch to the floor. Vases and knick-knacks fall with a crash. The water heater flips over, and a filing cabinet tips onto its front.

In an upstairs bedroom, the shaking is even worse. An entire bookshelf collapses. A bed shakes so much that it moves away from the wall and into the middle of the room.

In less than 15 seconds, the quaking ends. The small house seems okay—no broken walls or collapsed ceilings. But inside, the rooms are a junkyard of tossed furniture and broken glass.

Fortunately, this earthquake was very localized. It took place inside a laboratory at the University of California at San Diego. Engineers there had built the house on a large shake table. Shake tables allow researchers to observe and experiment with how buildings perform during earthquakes.

The testers used the shake table and computers to simulate the power and motion of the 1994 Northridge earthquake in California. That quake registered a magnitude of 6.7. It caused more than

A 2007 earthquake in Japan ripped apart this road. Collapsing roads, bridges, buildings, and other structures are the biggest killers during an earthquake. In addition, repair costs often run into the billions of dollars.

$40 billion in property damage, one of the costliest disasters in U.S. history. Yet only 61 people were killed. Fortunately, the quake hit at 4:30 A.M. before people were on the road to work or school. Good construction also played a part in keeping people safe.

There is a saying in earthquake science: "Earthquakes don't kill people; buildings kill people." In other words, collapsing buildings and falling objects are the biggest threat during an earthquake, not the heaving ground. That is why people are told to stand in a doorway, or crawl under a desk or heavy table, the instant they feel a tremor. These are two of the safest places inside any building during an earthquake. People outdoors are instructed to move away from places where bricks or other debris might come crashing down.

Constructing better, safer buildings is the most important action that communities in earthquake zones can take. It may never be possible to predict when a quake will hit. But smart disaster planning and sound construction have the potential to save many, many lives.

Building in the Danger Zone

Los Angeles, California. Seattle, Washington. Tokyo, Japan. Lima, Peru. Mexico City, Mexico. Istanbul, Turkey. These are some of the most-populated cities in the world. All have grown up and spread out rapidly, despite their locations in quake-prone regions. But sooner or later, all of them will take a hit from a catastrophic earthquake. It is just a matter of time before a "Big One" strikes each one of them.

Today, more people live in earthquake zones than ever before. Many come for work and other opportunities. Others may love an area's natural beauty and good weather. Near volcanoes, farmers might set down roots in the rich, volcanic soil.

In Pakistan, poor construction contributed to the deaths of thousands during a 2005 earthquake. Millions more were left homeless.

FAMILY SURVIVAL KIT

The Federal Emergency Management Administration (FEMA) is the government agency responsible for helping U.S. communities when disasters hit. FEMA recommends that every family put together a Disaster Supply Kit. The idea is that families will have what they need to go three days without electricity, running water, or access to supermarkets or other stores.

The disaster kit should be set aside where no one will raid it for snacks or other things. Then it will be ready to go if an earthquake or other disaster strikes.

Here is some of what FEMA suggests families put in their kit (For the complete list, go to http://www.fema.gov/kids/dizkit.htm.):

Water—There is no guarantee that pipes won't break or electricity will be available to pump water. That's why there should be enough bottled water so that each person has one gallon per day, plus extra for pets.

Food—There should be enough food to last for three days. The menu might include canned meat, fruit, vegetables, juice, milk, and soup; high-energy foods like peanut butter, granola bars, and nuts; fun foods like candy and cookies; and special food for babies, if necessary. All of these foods should be able to last without refrigeration.

First Aid Kit—This should include adhesive bandages, pain relievers, and other medical supplies.

Tools and Supplies—The toolkit should contain a flashlight, matches, candles, whistle, toilet paper, can opener, battery-powered radio, Swiss Army knife, and other equipment. These should be packed in a backpack in case people are forced to leave their home.

Clothing and Bedding—Everyone in the house should have sturdy shoes and a complete change of clothes ready and waiting. Equipment should also include raingear, warm underwear, and blankets or sleeping bags.

Human beings have short memories, for better or worse. An area may not experience a major earthquake or a volcanic eruption for many, many years—even centuries. People then tend to forget the instant destruction and death these seismic events can cause. They may stop taking the threat seriously and therefore build carelessly.

If a quake-prone community has the commitment and resources, though, it will build earthquake safety into its structures and streets. Its government will pass and enforce strict **building codes**. These are laws and standards that make sure construction is done properly. People need to know that their home or office won't collapse during a strong earthquake.

In poorer countries, many communities simply lack the resources or know-how to build safely. In many parts of the Middle East, Central Asia, and South America, people use whatever material is available: mud bricks, stone, adobe, or concrete. These materials are very solid and heavy, but also brittle and inflexible. Most structures are not reinforced with steel rods and other supports that would make them safer. During an earthquake, these

An earthquake demolished these buildings in Mexico City. In the future, smarter designs and better construction may reduce the destruction in quake-prone cities.

homes may crumble without warning, trapping or killing families inside. Multi-story buildings may "pancake"—each floor dropping onto the next.

The result is a high death toll. In October 2005, approximately 73,000 people died in the country of Pakistan, victims of a magnitude 7.6 quake. Nearly 4 million people were left homeless. Afterward, researchers found that more than half the buildings in the region were built of un-reinforced concrete block. The earthquake destroyed 60% of these buildings. Many children died when their poorly built schools fell on them.

"Most loss of life and property has been due to the collapse of [old] and unsafe structures," said seismologist Charles Richter, creator of the Richter scale. "In every area of the world where there is earthquake risk, there are still many buildings of this type; it is very frustrating to try to get rid of them."

Building Smart, Not Strong

In the fairy tale "The Three Little Pigs," the solid brick house foils The Big Bad Wolf. The straw and wood houses cannot stand up to his huffing and puffing.

When it comes to foiling earthquakes, the opposite is true. Flexibility is often more important than strength in creating structures that can withstand side-to-side shaking. If a house or other building can sway a little, it is more likely to survive. Wood-frame houses can often ride out a medium-sized shock because of their flexibility.

Steel also has qualities that make it hold up well during an earthquake. If bent slightly, steel can snap back. If twisted severely, it will bend but usually not break. For these reasons, steel rods are often sealed into concrete walls. These rods reinforce the concrete to keep it from collapsing in a disaster.

Basic construction improvements can reduce home damage and physical hazards in an earthquake zone. First, careful builders bolt the house to its concrete base, called the foundation. This keeps the house from slipping during a quake. Chimneys should also be secured to reduce their chances of falling. Inside, home-owners should batten down water heaters, refrigerators, and top-heavy furniture to keep them from tipping over. Stores in quake zones often put up special shelves that keep bottles from falling to the floor.

For houses built of brick, adobe, or other rigid material, engineers recommend that the walls be reinforced with fiber mesh. Steel rods can be built into the walls. The roof, ceiling, and walls should be strapped together with steel straps so that they reinforce each other.

In many communities, building codes require these safeguards in new homes. Experts, though, worry about older houses. They strongly suggest that homeowners upgrade their property so that it can withstand earthquake damage. The improvements may even save their families' lives.

ON SOLID GROUND

The ground a structure is built on has a lot to do with how well it can handle an earthquake. If it is anchored in solid ground or rock, it has a better chance of surviving a major shock.

Many cities, though, have grown up on unstable ground. Often loose dirt and rock called landfill are hauled in and dumped to create a building site. Sometimes developers create land by pouring rock, sand, and dirt into water to increase the building area. This usually presents few problems—as long as the earth remains still.

When an earthquake hits, though, the problem gets big very quickly. Strong quaking shakes apart the loose soil, especially if it's wet. The ground then becomes like quicksand. Buildings perched on such an area may tilt or even topple over as the ground shakes and settles unevenly beneath them.

To make matters worse, soft soil intensifies an earthquake's shaking. If a person hits a boulder with a big stick, for example, someone sitting on the boulder nearby may not even notice. But if a person taps a bowl of Jell-O, the Jell-O will wiggle crazily. In a similar way, loose ground will shake with extra violence during a quake.

Structures need to be both strong and flexible in order to survive earthquakes. Engineers retrofitted this building in Vancouver, Canada, with steel braces to help it withstand shocks.

High-rise buildings and skyscrapers present unique challenges when it comes to earthquake safety. They need to be flexible enough to sway a little. At the same time, they need to be stiff enough so that they do not whip violently back and forth.

Changes made at Los Angeles City Hall include several engineering advancements. Built in 1928, the building was badly damaged in the 1994 Northridge earthquake. Afterward, the building was strengthened with steel braces and bars. These helped reinforce the building's stone walls and central tower.

Engineers also dug down and put a suspension system beneath the building. It includes shock absorbers made of rubber and steel. This assembly acts like the suspension in a car. It cushions the building when the ground moves and will absorb some of the shock when a quake hits.

Scientists and engineers are also teaming up to develop "smart buildings" for the future. These structures would include a computerized system. In response to a quake, the computers would sense the direction and intensity of the destructive waves. Then the system would automatically tighten and loosen different joints to allow the building to protect itself.

Buildings are not the only structures that require attention. Highway bridges and overpasses, for example, can also collapse during a quake. They have a better chance to remain standing if their columns are reinforced with extra steel and anchored deep in the ground. Another improvement involves constructing underground tunnels with flexible joints. That way a tunnel can wiggle and twist without snapping. This improvement would help protect water pipes, electric and gas lines, and subway systems during a quake.

Preparing for an earthquake or other natural disaster is truly a team effort. Government officials, scientists, engineers, phone and power repair crews, emergency workers, and citizens must all work together. They must practice how they will react when the "Big One" hits. Because when it does, they will not have time to fumble around figuring out what to do.

CHAPTER SIX

The Probability of Predicting Disaster

I t was going to hit sometime between 1984 and 1992. That was the period of time a team of scientists believed an earthquake would rock the ground near the small town of Parkfield, California. Scientific research showed that magnitude 6.0 or higher shocks had shaken that area regularly. Now researchers were trying to calculate the next big thumping.

They were hopeful that close monitoring would help identify **precursors**. These are signs that the fault is about to break loose and release its earthshaking energy. If they could spot before-quake clues, perhaps it would help them better predict future shocks.

They zeroed in on 1988, plus or minus four years. They set up seismometers, **tiltmeters**, and other sensors. They measured movement in the Earth's crust. They monitored the water levels and other details.

They waited—1988 came and went. And waited—1992 came and went. The quake they were watching for finally struck in 2004.

Afterward, researchers studied all the readings from the sensors. They searched for some hint that the earthquake had been about to happen. To their frustration, they found nothing. The quake had hit without any warning that they could see.

To monitor earth-
quakes, seismologists
use sophisticated
equipment like this
seismograph. Seis-
mographs measure
and record the seis-
mic waves that rip-
ple out from a
quake's epicenter.
Most seismographs
today use computer
screen displays
instead of paper.

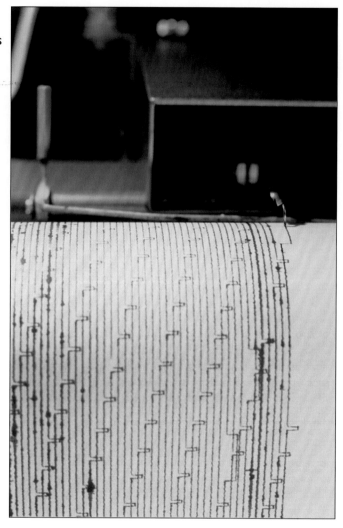

Like meteorologists predicting a storm, earth scientists wish they could foretell earthquakes and other seismic events. But most seismologists believe that specific, reliable earthquake forecasting lies decades in the future. Some believe it may never be possible. That's because the tectonic plates that cause quakes interact in a very complex fashion. Countless factors go into what happens as the plates push against and squeeze past each other.

Still, seismology remains a very young science. Every year, new knowledge and better technology help earth scientists better understand why and where the ground shakes and volcanoes erupt.

The Search for Earthquake Precursors

In the days or hours before a major earthquake hits, people sometimes report unusual details. Water from their wells suddenly tastes bad, or they see strange lights in the sky. Their pets or farm animals become nervous or frantic.

For years, scientists have sorted through such information for common clues about when an earthquake is about to let loose. So far, they have found nothing reliable.

The most common earthquake precursor is foreshocks. These smaller quakes may precede the mainshock. Most often, though, a small earthquake is just a small earthquake. Fewer than one out of twenty small earthquakes is followed by a mainshock.

In at least one case, though, everyday observations helped alert people about a coming quake. In 1975, Haicheng, China, suffered hundreds of small tremors. Water levels in wells fell. People reported strange animal behavior. Hibernating snakes, for example, were said to have awakened and slithered out of their holes. Officials had told people that such signs might predict a coming quake.

Officials evacuated the area. The decision paid off when a magnitude 7.4 quake struck. Few lives were lost.

Chinese officials and scientists congratulated themselves. They thought that, perhaps, they had found a practical way to predict big earthquakes. But they were mistaken. Less than a year later another quake hit near Tangshan. This time no one noticed anything unusual beforehand. No evacuation took place and more than 250,000 people died. The conclusion: earthquake precursors rarely, if ever, follow recognizable patterns.

Stress-Triggering

One **hypothesis**, or theory, may be helping earth scientists explore how some faults behave and interact, however. They call the idea "stress triggering."

Earthquakes occur when a stuck fault suddenly breaks free. At that point the ground releases stress. But the stress-triggering theory suggests that the stress does not simply disappear. Some of it transfers to nearby faults or to another part of the same fault. This idea helped earth scientists recognize an earthquake threat in Turkey.

In August 1999, a stretch of the North Anatolian Fault slipped there. The resulting magnitude 7.4 quake rocked the city of Izmit to the ground. Concrete buildings collapsed in clouds of gray dust, killing some 25,000 people. It was the twelfth major shock to strike along that fault since 1939.

A group of earth scientists had noticed a pattern in the quakes. Each shock seemed to strike farther west along the fault. The scientists, including geologist Aykut A. Barka, suspected that each quake had transferred stress to the next section of the fault. This would increase the chances of a quake happening there. If they were right, they figured that the next earthquake would strike

CAN FIDO FORECAST DISASTER?

The December 2004 tsunami killed tens of thousands of people in Asia. One of the countries hardest hit was Sri Lanka. Yet wildlife officials there noticed something odd. They found few dead wild animals in the disaster's aftermath. There were also reports in Thailand about how some work elephants grew agitated that day. They stamped their feet, broke their chains, and fled before the tsunami hit.

Scientists have long wondered if animals have unique abilities to sense coming disaster. History features many tales about dogs howling and birds falling silent before a large earthquake hits. Perhaps animals feel sudden changes in air pressure or in Earth's electromagnetic field, experts have speculated. Perhaps keen animal hearing or super-sensitivity to vibrations alerts them to dangers before humans know something is wrong.

Most of these stories, though, are anecdotal. That means that they are based on personal stories, not on scientific research. A team of scientists at Japan's University of Osaka is trying to change that. In their lab, they are closely watching catfish to see if they change behavior shortly before an earthquake. But so far, any hope for reliable animal earthquake predictors remains unproven.

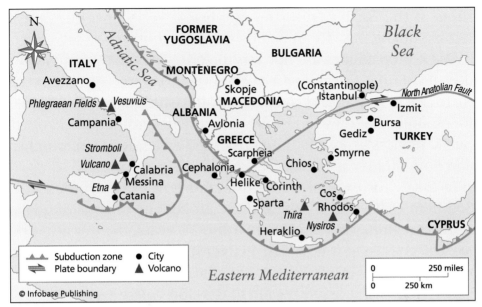

This map of the eastern Mediterranean Sea shows the plate boundaries and subduction zones of that region. Knowing where faults occur helps scientists and government officials know what places are at greatest risk of damage.

about 65 miles (100 km) to the west of Izmit. They marked a likely spot near the city of Düzce.

They did not have long to wait. Just three months after the Izmit quake, a magnitude 7.1 shock hit near Düzce.

Fortunately, Barka had published his findings before that quake hit. He noted the risk that Düzce faced. Engineers there had taken the warning to heart. They closed school buildings that had been slightly damaged by the Izmit quake. Officials complained that the students had nowhere else to study. But the engineers held firm and were proven right. Some of the damaged school buildings collapsed in the quake. Barka's efforts may have saved many lives.

For the foreseeable future, though, earthquakes will likely remain beyond reliable prediction. What earth scientists can do is calculate a long time period for when and where a quake may strike. Within that period, they can estimate the probability, or chances, of a major shock occurring. They do this by analyzing stress in the Earth's crust, the number of years since the fault's last big quake, activity in nearby faults, and other factors.

These probabilities are not very precise. They may stretch over decades of time. Seismologists may never be able to say, "This week there is a 50% chance of a magnitude 6.0 earthquake in our area," for example. But they can let fire departments, hospitals, and other public services assess the future risk their area faces. Communities and households can then decide how best to prepare.

In 2007, for example, scientists and government officials in Southern California announced the probability of a major quake in their region. They said that within 30 years, there was a 30% to 70% chance of a very destructive shock near Los Angeles. To raise awareness of the threat, they launched the "Dare to Prepare" program. It asked people to develop emergency plans and pack disaster kits for their families.

If no major quake hits the area within 30 years, people may shake their heads and complain that the experts were wrong. But if the "Big One" does hit, the public will thank earth scientists for the heads up. The value of being prepared must outweigh irritation about an incorrect prediction.

Monitoring Volcanic Eruptions

In 1985, the eruption of Nevado del Ruiz in Colombia set off a massive lahar, or mudslide. The wall of mud and debris wiped out town of Armero, killing more than 22,000 people. In response, the United States Geological Survey formed the Volcano Disaster Assistance Program (VDAP). This team of volcanologists stands ready to jet to stirring volcanoes around the world. They carry with them the latest in technological equipment.

Once on-site, VDAP joins with local scientists to watch closely for signs of a coming eruption. They also assist local officials in creating emergency plans, including plans for evacuating people in the area. This program has saved thousands of lives already.

Usually, volcanic eruptions offer more precursors than earthquakes do. That means volcanologists can gather more clues about

Remote monitors aid researchers in keeping track of volcanic and seismic activity. The device pictured here allows scientists to check volcanic gases for changes that might signal a coming eruption.

what is going on inside a volcano's guts. Most critical, they watch for signs that magma is on the move. To do this, they may plant a network of sensors on the volcano's flanks. With the threat of an eruption at any moment, this can be scary and even deadly work.

The sensors spy on three aspects of a volcano's behavior. One is seismic activity. Portable seismometers are placed to feel and measure small earthquakes caused by moving magma. "Shallow volcanic earthquakes are perhaps the most frequent and reliable sign that a volcano is about to burst back into life," writes volcanologist Alwyn Scarth.

Researchers may also hook up temperature and chemical sensors. Rising heat may mean magna is nearing the surface. And a change in the gases the volcano releases may also signal danger. Levels of carbon dioxide, sulfur dioxide, and hydrogen sulfide will usually increase before an eruption.

Thirdly, volcanologists may set up tiltmeters. These devices can sense tiny changes in the shape of the ground. Often, parts of a volcano will bulge or collapse as a precursor to eruptions.

More and more, volcanologists rely on satellite monitoring of volcanoes. Sophisticated instruments can measure changes of temperature from orbits high above Earth. By placing markers on the volcano, researchers can also use the global positioning system, or GPS, to watch for telltale changes in the volcano's shape. (GPS is a network of satellites that can pinpoint a surface location within inches.)

To date, the eruption of Pinatubo in the Philippines stands out as the most glowing success of volcanology and VDAP. Scientists estimated that this volcano had not erupted in 400 to 600 years. But in April 1991, it began showing signs of life. Some 15,000 people farmed this stratovolcano's fertile slopes. Another half million lived in the surrounding area. All were at risk from a major eruption. Philippine volcanologists and VDAP gathered to judge the danger.

In May 1991, the Philippine Institute of Volcanology published a hazard map. This map highlighted the areas most at risk from lahars, pyroclastic flows, and ashfall. TV stations also repeatedly broadcast a show about volcanic threats. These educational efforts informed the public about what it faced and readied them for action.

That same month, seismometers measured about 1,800 small earthquakes. Chemical sensors picked up a 1,000% increase in sulfur dioxide gas. On June 6, a tiltmeter signaled that the summit was bulging out at a faster rate. The signs added up to the possibility of a major eruption. The monitoring team recommended a mass evacuation, and local officials put their plan in motion. More than 100,000 people left the danger zone.

Pinatubo experienced a series of short eruptions in the second week of June. Then on June 15, the mountain blew nearly 1,000 feet (300 m) off its top. It sent a thundercloud of ash more than

6 miles (10 km) into the sky. Pyroclastic flows blasted from the mountain's sides. Lahars flowed down the river valleys.

The death toll, though, only numbered in the hundreds. Many of these victims died when their roofs collapsed from the weight of falling ash. Many thousands more might have died without the close cooperation of these scientists and public officials.

Pinatubo, Mount St. Helens, and other volcanoes gave clear warnings that they would soon erupt. At the same time, supposedly extinct volcanoes may give no hint that they are alive—

The 1991 eruption of Pinatubo in the Philippines covered the region in ash. The ash fall caused the deaths of dozens of people when their roofs collapsed on top of them.

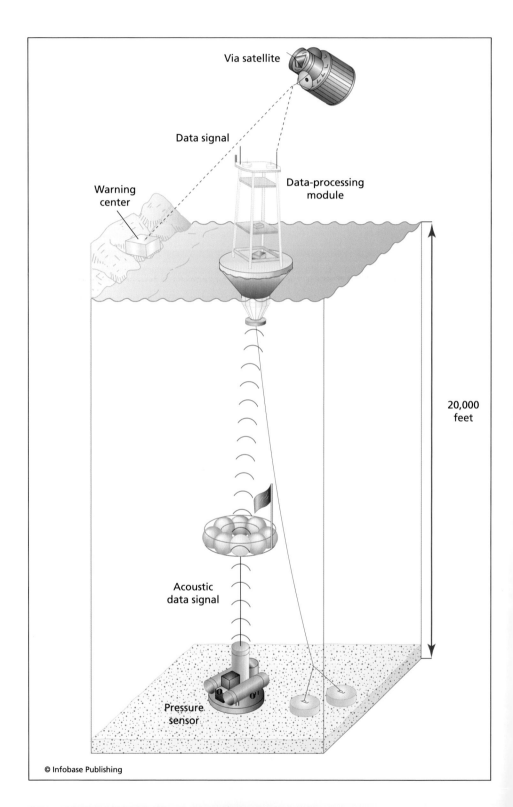

Via satellite

Data signal

Data-processing module

Warning center

20,000 feet

Acoustic data signal

Pressure sensor

© Infobase Publishing

until they explode. Since 1900, more than a dozen volcanoes have violently erupted without any previous sign that they were active. Volcanologists argue that this offers the best reason to expand and improve the monitoring of volcanoes worldwide.

Sensing Tsunamis

There was no tsunami-warning system in place in the Indian Ocean on December 26, 2004. That was the day a huge earthquake sent a tsunami charging at Asian coastlines.

The lack of such a system contributed to the deaths of some 220,000 people across the Indian Ocean. For those on Sumatra, the large island nearest the huge tsunami-causing quake, the killer waves arrived too fast for any alert to have done much good. But for other coastal countries, the tsunami took two to three hours to reach their shores. For them, a warning system could have saved thousands of lives.

Underwater earthquakes trigger most tsunamis, as mentioned earlier. So quake detection is often the first hint that a tsunami may be on its way. That is why a network of earthquake sensors is an important feature in tsunami prediction. But for people who live near an underwater quake's epicenter, their best hope is to run for high ground as soon as they feel a strong tremor.

At the same time, scientists are hurrying to set up a reliable network of tsunami-sensing equipment in the Indian Ocean. Such a system is already operating in the Pacific Ocean. This system includes placing tsunami-sensing technology in the deep ocean. The farther from shore a tsunami is spied, the more warning coastlines will have.

This high-tech system includes a buoy anchored to the deep-ocean floor. The buoy is linked to a pressure sensor, also planted

(opposite): This is a diagram of a deep-sea tsunami sensor. The pressure sensor on the seafloor can sense a tsunami's unique wave pattern. A satellite then relays the information to a warning center.

on the ocean floor. This pressure sensor has the ability to distinguish more powerful tsunami waves from the ocean's normal wave action.

If the sensor does identify a tsunami, it sends a signal to the buoy floating on the ocean surface. The buoy contains a satellite uplink that can instantly alert scientists to the danger. Scientists can then communicate the danger to coastline areas.

The weak link in the system may be getting the message to communities in a tsunami's path. As the 2004 tsunami demonstrated, many coastal villages are poor and lack modern communications. This shortcoming will have to improve for tsunami-warning systems to be widely effective.

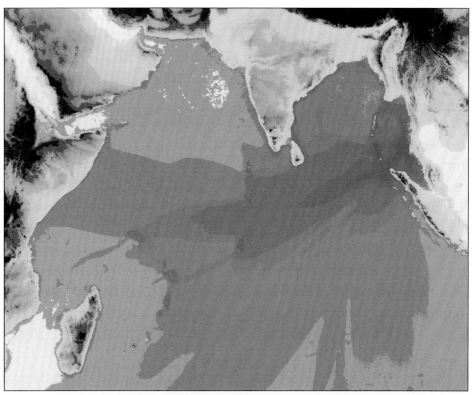

This image is a computer simulation of the December 26, 2004 tsunami. The darker pink areas in the Indian Ocean indicate the tallest waves. Powerful computers are helping scientists understand and predict the behavior of tsunamis, earthquakes, and volcanoes.

COMPUTER QUAKES

Scientists cannot study earthquakes under microscopes or constantly observe them as they do wild animals. Quakes strike and stop, often without warning. And they usually last less than a minute. For seismologists, this makes quakes very difficult to study.

To get around this problem, Earth scientists program supercomputers to create computer models of quake-prone areas. Using math formulas and maps, they try to recreate faults and how they act. They input millions of math equations and data from scientific research that tell the model what to do. When a real earthquake hits, they take measurements from it and add it to the model to improve accuracy.

Computer models allow researchers to study how one fault might add stress to another fault. They can also predict how a quake will affect a city or region.

Earth scientists also use computer models to study volcanoes and tsunamis. In time, experts hope that creating these artificial disasters will give them the power to predict and prepare for real ones.

Humans will never have the power to stop volcanoes, earthquakes, and tsunamis from unleashing their destructive power. But good research can help scientists reduce the number of catastrophic surprises.

Still, the restless Earth will always be full of surprises. Thus, the most useful response to seismic threats remains preparation. Being prepared means that people learn the risks facing their communities. It means the dependable construction of buildings so that they will stay standing when the earth shakes. It means maintaining well-trained fire departments and other emergency services to come to the rescue when disaster does strike.

Being prepared closer to home means families, schools, and businesses developing emergency plans and packing disaster kits. It means practicing emergency drills so that people know what to do. In these ways, scientists, community leaders, and the public can team up when the Earth gets restless.

Glossary

asthenosphere – semi-fluid layer of mantle on which the Earth's tectonic plates slowly move

building codes – construction rules and standards

calderas – large hollows caused by the explosion or collapse of a volcano

composite volcano – *see* "stratovolcano"

continental drift – the theory that Earth's continents split off from one supercontinent and slowly moved apart

convection – a pattern of circulation in which heated gas or liquid rises before cooling and sinking

core – the center part of Earth, thought to consist of superheated metal

crust – the surface layer of Earth

epicenter – a spot on the Earth's surface directly above an earthquake's focus

eruption – release of gases and lava from a volcano

evacuate – to leave a dangerous place for a safer location

fault – the boundary between tectonic plates

focus – the spot underground where a fault breaks free, causing an earthquake

friction – the force that slows movement and produces heat when two surfaces rub

geologist – a scientist who studies the earth and its life, especially as it is recorded in rocks

hot spot – the area in the center of a tectonic plate where magma burns through, forming a volcano

hypothesis – an educated prediction

lahar – a flash flood and mudslide caused by a volcano

lava – melted rock that comes out of a volcano and hardens

magma – melted rock beneath or within the Earth's crust

magnitude – a measurement for gauging the power of an earthquake

mantle – the layer between the Earth's core and crust

plate tectonics – the theory that the Earth's crust is made of moving sections

precursor – a sign that an earthquake, volcanic eruption, or other disaster is about to happen

primary, or **P wave** – the fastest body wave of an earthquake that compresses and expands the earth

pyroclastic flow – an avalanche of lava and hot gases from a volcanic eruption

Richter scale – a system for measuring the energy released by an earthquake

secondary, or S-wave – the second-fastest seismic body wave that moves sharply up and down or sideways

seafloor spreading – the place where two tectonic plates are moving apart, and lava is forming new ocean floor

sediment – deposits of sand, rocks, and other material that were carried by water

seismic wave – the vibration from an earthquake that passes through the earth

seismometer – an instrument for detecting and measuring earthquakes

seismologist – a scientist who analyzes earthquakes

stratovolcano – steep-sided volcanic cone

subduction zone – an area where one tectonic plate is dragged down under another tectonic plate

surface wave – a slow seismic wave that ripples out along the earth's surface

tectonic plate – a giant segment of rock within the Earth's crust

tiltmenter – an instrument that detects small changes in the ground's shape

volcano – an opening in the Earth's crust where hot gases and melted rock escape from the mantle

Bibliography

Achenbach, Joel. "The Next Big One." *National Geographic.* April 2006, pp. 120–147.

Ballard, Robert D. *Exploring Our Living Planet.* Washington, D.C.: National Geographic Society, 1983.

Bindeman, Ilya N. "The Secrets of the Supervolcanoes." *Scientific American.* June 2006, pp. 36–43.

British Broadcasting Corporation. "Award for Tsunami Warning Pupil." BBC News Website, September 9, 2005. Available online at http://news.bbc.co.uk/2/hi/uk_news/4229392.stm.

Erickson, Jon. *Volcanoes and Earthquakes.* Blue Ridge Summit, Pa.: TAB Books, Inc., 1988.

Geist, Eric L., et al. "Tsunami: Wave of Change." *Scientific American.* January 2006, pp. 56–63.

González, Frank I. "Tsunami!" *Scientific American.* May 1999, pp. 56–65.

Hough, Susan Elizabeth. *Earthshaking Science.* Princeton, N.J.: Princeton University Press, 2002.

Kious, W. Jacqueline and Robert I. Tilling. *This Dynamic Earth: The Story of Plate Tectonics.* USGS Special Interest Publication, 1996.

Klampe, Michelle L. "Southern Californians urged: Prepare for a really big quake." Scripps-McClatchy Western Service, January 10, 2007.

Lambourne, Helen. "Tsunami: Anatomy of a Disaster," BBC News Online, March 27, 2005. Available online at http://news.bbc.co.uk/2/hi/science/nature/4381395.stm.

LeVay, Simon. "Riding the Rumble." *Scientific American.* October 2000, pp. 17–18.

Prager, Ellen J. *Furious Earth.* New York: McGraw Hill, 2000.

Ritchie, David and Alexander E. Gates. *Encyclopedia of Earthquakes and Volcanoes.* New York: Checkmark Books, 2001.

Scarth, Alwyn. *Volcanoes.* College Station, Tex.: Texas A & M Press, 1994.

Stein, Ross S. "Earthquake Conversations." *Scientific American.* January 2003, pp. 72–79.

The Virtual Museum of the City of San Francisco. "The Great 1906 Earthquake and Fire." Available online at www.sfmuseum.org/1906/06.html.

Walker, Bryce. *Earthquake.* Alexandria, Va.: Time-Life Books, 1982.

Further Exploration

BOOKS

Bonar, Samantha. *Tsunamis*. Mankato, Minn.: Capstone Press, 2006.

DK Publishing. *Eyewitness: Volcano & Earthquake*. New York: DK Publishing, 2004.

Ganeri, Anita. *Violent Volcanoes and Earth-Shattering Earthquakes*. New York: Scholastic, 2006.

Johnson, Rebecca L. *Plate Tectonics*. Minneapolis, Minn.: Lerner Books, 2006.

Rosi, Mauro, et al. *Volcanoes*. Buffalo, N.Y.: Firefly Books Ltd., 2003.

Simon, Seymour. *Earthquakes*. New York: HarperCollins, 2006. Princeton, N.J.: Princeton University Press, 2002.

Stille, Darlene R. *Plate Tectonics: Earth's Moving Crust*. Mankato, Minn.: Compass Point Books, 2007.

Torres, John Albert. *Disaster in the Indian Ocean: Tsunami 2004*. Hockessin, Del.: Mitchell Lane Publishers, 2005.

Townsend, John. *Earthquakes And Volcanoes – a Survival Guide: Earth's Physical Processes*. Chicago, Ill.: Raintree, 2006.

WEB SITES

www.enchantedlearning.com/subjects/astronomy/planets/earth/Continents.shtml
Plate tectonics—animated

www.pbs.org/wnet/savageearth/index.html
The Public Broadcasting Station's site explores plate tectonics, volcanoes, earthquakes, and tsunamis—animated

http://earthquake.usgs.gov/learning/students.php
Interactive earthquake hazards program, maintained by the United States Geological Survey

http://volcano.und.edu/
Up-to-date information on volcanic activity, plus volcano-related facts and activities

http://homeschooling.gomilpitas.com/explore/tsunami.htm
Science of tsunamis

Index

About the Author

Sean McCollum is an award-winning author of 20 nonfiction books for children and teens. He is a regular contributor to *National Geographic Kids, Boys' Life*, and Scholastic. He is also a writing instructor at Front Range Community College in Colorado. A traveler to about 50 countries, McCollum has yet to experience an earthquake or a tsunami but has hiked to the top of several volcanoes.

Picture Credits

PAGE: 3: Stephen & Donna O'Meara/Photo Researchers, Inc.
    8: Ragnar Larusson/Photo Researchers, Inc.
    10: Krafft/Photo Researchers, Inc.
    11: © Infobase Publishing
    14: Dr. Ken MacDonald/Photo Researchers, Inc.
    15: © Infobase Publishing
    17: © Infobase Publishing
    19: Lee Battaglia/Photo Researchers, Inc.
    21: Bernhard Edmaier/Photo Researchers, Inc.
    22: © Infobase Publishing
    24: United States Geological Survey
    26: © Infobase Publishing
    27: © Infobase Publishing
    28: Explorer/Photo Researchers, Inc.
    30: United States Geological Survey
    32: Corbis/Bettmann
    35: David Parker/Photo Researchers, Inc.
    36: © Infobase Publishing
    37: © Infobase Publishing
    38: AP Images/William J. Smith
    42: AP Images/Eugene Hoshiko
    44: © Infobase Publishing
    45: © Salamanderman/Shutterstock
    47: © Infobase Publishing
    48: David Hardy/Photo Researchers, Inc.
    51: AP Images/Koji Sasahara
    52: AP Images/Tomas Munita
    54: Wesley Bocxe/Photo Researchers, Inc.
    57: Fletcher and Baylis/Photo Researchers, Inc.
    60: James King-Holmes/Photo Researchers, Inc.
    63: © Infobase Publishing
    65: Philippe Bourseiller/Photo Researchers, Inc.
    67: Mauro Fermariello/Photo Researchers, Inc.
    68: © Infobase Publishing
    70: Yalciner, Kuran, Taymaz/Photo Researchers, Inc.

COVER (LEFT TO RIGHT):

Mt. St. Helens in Washington State spews smoke and ash into the sky in April 1980. (AP Images/Jack Smith)

A tsunami hits the shore in Ao Nang, Krabi Province, Thailand during the 2004 Indian Ocean Earthquake and Tsunami. (© David Rydevik)

A road cracked by earthquakes in the town of Solok in Indonesia's West Sumatra province on March 7, 2007. (Reuters/Muhammad Fitrah/Landov)